I·N·S·I·D·E
GREAT BRITAIN

Ian James

Photography: Chris Fairclough

Franklin Watts
London · New York · Sydney · Toronto

CONTENTS

© 1988 Franklin Watts
12a Golden Square
London W1

Published in the USA by
Franklin Watts Inc.
387 Park Avenue South
New York, N.Y. 10016

Franklin Watts Australia
14 Mars Road
Lane Cove
NSW 2066

Design: Edward Kinsey
Illustrations: Hayward Art Group

UK ISBN: 0 86313 710 5
US ISBN: 0 531 10612 8
Library of Congress Catalog
Card Number 88-50194

Phototypset by Lineage, Watford
Printed in Belgium

Additional photographs:
Michael Halford 7, 8, 22;
Poperfoto 9 (T), 29 (T)

Front cover: Chris Fairclough
Back cover: Chris Fairclough

The land

Great Britain is a large island lying off the coast of mainland Europe. It contains three countries: England, Scotland and Wales. It also includes many small offshore islands, such as the Isle of Wight in England, the Hebrides in Scotland and Anglesey in Wales.

The main highlands are in the north and west. The highlands of northern Scotland contain Britain's highest peak, Ben Nevis, which is 1,343 m (4,406 ft) above sea level. Central Scotland is low-lying, but southern Scotland consists largely of rounded hills. Wales is also mountainous. Mount Snowdon reaches 1,085 m (3,560 ft) in North Wales. Great Britain's longest river, the Severn, rises in Wales. It is 354 km (220 miles) long.

Below: **The beautiful coast of the Gower peninsula in South Wales.**

Above: **The Lake District in northwestern England is a national park.**

Left: **Turville in Buckinghamshire is a typical English village set in rolling countryside.**

Northern England contains two upland regions: the Pennine chain and the Lake District. Southwestern England is a tableland, with rocky outcrops and windswept moorland. Fertile lowlands, separated by low chalk and limestone hills, cover much of England. The flattest area is called the Fens. This area surrounds the Wash, an inlet of the North Sea.

Great Britain has a mainly mild, changeable climate. The wettest areas are the western highlands, where many places have an average yearly rainfall of more than 200 cm (79 inches), while the east coast has less than 76 cm (30 inches). Average temperatures increase from north to south.

Above: **The Scottish Highlands contain many lakes, called lochs.**

The people and their history

Throughout history, many people have settled in Great Britain. As a result, the island has a mixed population. Early arrivals included the Celts, who began to settle more than 2,500 years ago. Celtic languages include Cornish, Irish, Scots Gaelic and Welsh.

The Romans ruled the south between the first and early fifth centuries. The Romans founded an orderly society, though they never conquered the north. When they left, the island was invaded by Germanic peoples, including the Angles, Saxons and Jutes. The English language is based on Germanic languages. Later invaders of Great Britain included Vikings, or Norsemen. The last time the country was invaded was in 1066. The invaders were the Normans, who were the descendants of Vikings living in France.

Below: **The Bayeux Tapestry tells the story of the Norman Conquest of England in 1066.**

Above: **A painting showing the defeat of the Spanish Armada by the English in 1588.**

England conquered Wales in 1282 and the two countries became united. A law uniting England and Wales with Scotland was passed in 1707.

England's power was based on its navy. In 1588, it defeated the Spanish Armada (fleet), preventing an invasion. British power steadily increased and in the late 18th century, Great Britain was the first to become an industrial country. By the mid-19th century, Great Britain was the world's richest country. It ruled the biggest empire in history. Britain became a haven for immigrants. Many of them, including Jews, had been persecuted in their homelands.

Two World Wars weakened Britain and, between 1947 and 1980, nearly all of the country's colonies became independent. Some citizens from the old colonies settled in Great Britain.

Above: **London and other cities were badly damaged by bombing in World War II.**

Right: **British people now come from many different ethnic and cultural backgrounds.**

9

Towns and cities

By world standards, Great Britain is a crowded place. About 92 per cent of its people live in cities and towns. In Europe, only Belgium has a higher percentage of people in urban areas.

Most highland areas are thinly populated. But some parts of the lowlands, especially in southeastern, central and northern England are among the world's most thickly populated places. England's largest cities are Greater London (population, 6,775,000), Birmingham (1,004,000), Leeds (711,000) and Sheffield (534,000). Glasgow (725,000) and Edinburgh (438,000), Scotland's capital, are the largest cities in Scotland's thickly populated central lowlands. Cardiff (280,000) is the capital and largest city in Wales.

Below: **Shamley Green is a village in Surrey.**

Right: **Edinburgh Castle overlooks Scotland's capital city.**

Below: **Most towns, such as Newbury in Southern England, have one main shopping area.**

Most British cities started to grow after the Industrial Revolution began in the late 18th century. Some cities were ports. Others built were on coalfields or in places where water power could be used to run machines.

Today, the central parts of many cities contain old houses. It is also expensive to live there, so many people have moved out into suburbs. Other people have settled in new towns. Since 1946, 21 new towns have been set up in England, 5 in Scotland and 2 in Wales. They have a total population of two million.

Many people have left country areas, because farms now depend on machines, not farmworkers. But some older people, who have retired from city jobs, are now settling in villages.

Above: **New towns and new parts of old cities, such as Bristol, shown here, are carefully planned.**

Right: **The map shows major cities and routes in Great Britain.**

Below: **A view of the Thames and the City of London, one of the world's great financial centres.**

Dundee
Aberdeen
Edinburgh
Glasgow

Newcastle
Sunderland
Teeside

York
Bradford
Leeds
Liverpool
Manchester
Sheffield
Wolverhampton
Nottingham
Birmingham
Coventry
Norwich
Ipswich
Swansea
Northampton
Cardiff
Oxford
London
Bristol
Bournemouth
Brighton
Southampton
Portsmouth

London is the capital of the United Kingdom of Great Britain and Northern Ireland. It contains the country's parliament – the elected House of Commons and the House of Lords. Britain is a monarchy and Buckingham Palace is the monarch's London home.

London, or Londinium, was a major Roman port on the River Thames. It has grown into one of the world's leading financial and commercial cities. London's Roman origins are still being uncovered. Other old buildings include the Tower of London, which was begun in 1079 by the Norman William the Conqueror. William was crowned in Westminster Abbey, one of Britain's finest churches, along with St. Paul's Cathedral. London suffered damage from a fire in 1666 and again in World War II.

Below: **A plan of central London.**
 1 **Royal Albert Hall**
 2 **Albert Memorial**
 3 **Wellington Arch**
 4 **Marble Arch**
 5 **Buckingham Palace**
 6 **Westminster Abbey**
 7 **Houses of Parliament**
 8 **Nelson's Column**
 9 **Statue of Eros**
10 **Post Office Tower**
11 **Cleopatra's Needle**
12 **Royal Festival Hall**
13 **St Paul's Cathedral**
14 **The Monument**
15 **Tower of London**
16 **Tower Bridge**

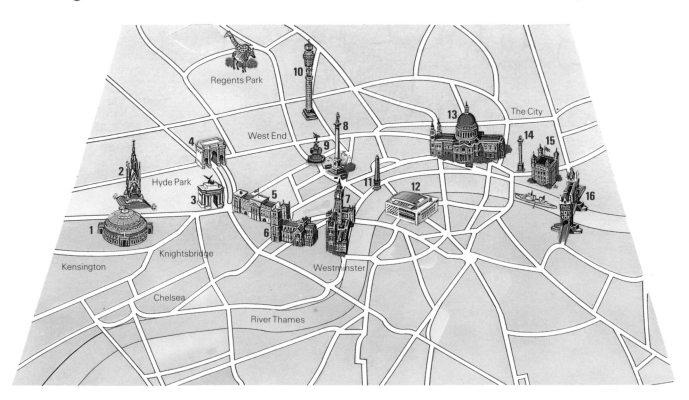

Family life

About 60 per cent of British households own or are buying their homes. About four out of every five families live in houses. Families are becoming smaller. The average family in 1911 contained more than four persons. By 1985, it was 2.56. This is partly because people now have fewer children and also because fewer elderly relatives now live with their children. Women do most of the work in the home. But 60 per cent of women between 16 and 60 now have jobs outside the home. As a result, men are playing a bigger role in running the home.

Living standards are rising. By 1985, over 90 per cent of homes had at least one television set and a refrigerator and 62 per cent had the use of a car (or van). The average life expectancy rose from 50 years in 1900 to 75 in 1985.

Below: **Many families now live on modern estates on the outskirts of towns.**

Right: **Family activities include card games.**

Below: **Watching television and listening to music are popular pastimes.**

Food

The British are famous for their roast meat, meat pies and milk puddings. Roast meat remains the chief feature of Sunday lunch, which is the chief meal of the week for may families. Some people like large breakfasts, including cereal, bacon and eggs, and toast with marmalade. But many people now prefer a light breakfast and a snack at lunchtime, with a cooked dinner in the evening.

On the average, Britons spend less on food than people in many other countries. Many people buy packaged, frozen and canned foods, because they are quick to prepare. Takeaway food, such as fish and chips, is popular. Today many restaurants also provide takeaway food.

Below: **Shops are offering an increasing variety of goods to cater for Britain's many cultures.**

Left: **On weekdays breakfast may be the only time some families eat together.**

Below: **Many people still preserve the customs and foods of their ancestors.**

Sports and pastimes

Britain's leading spectator sport is soccer, though rugby takes first place in some areas. Cricket is popular in summer. Many people enjoy horse racing, though the amount people spend on gambling has gone down in recent years. Fishing is a major activity, and swimming and walking are the two leading forms of exercise.

Most people spend the bulk of their leisure time at home. Television watching, reading and gardening all take up a lot of time. People over the age of four spend, on the average, 27 hours a week viewing television. Almost a third of homes have video recorders. About half of Britain's households have a pet. Dogs number more than six million. There are also almost as many cats.

Below: **Cricket has been a popular sport for more than 200 years.**

In 1963, most people had one annual vacation, lasting two weeks. Today 95 out of every 100 people can claim four weeks or more.

About three out of every five people take at least one long vacation away from home. In 1986, Britons took 31.5 million vacations in Britain. The top destinations were coastal resorts, though some people preferred to visit the country's beauty spots, including the ten national parks of England and Wales. These parks cover nine per cent of the area of England and Wales. Scotland has no national parks, though it has magnificent scenery.

In 1986, Britons also took about 17 million vacations abroad. The most popular countries were Spain, France and Greece.

Above: **Brighton, on England's south coast, is a major seaside resort.**

The arts

Literature has been Britain's leading art form. For example, the plays of William Shakespeare (1564-1616) and the novels of Charles Dickens (1812-1870) and the poetry of Scotland's national poet Robert Burns (1759-1796) are read around the world. Britain has produced many fine books for children. Masterpieces include *Robinson Crusoe* by Daniel Defoe (1660-1731), *The Adventures of Alice in Wonderland* by Lewis Carroll (1832-1898).

British architecture is also well known, especially its great churches. The Norman style began following the Norman conquest of 1066, and the Gothic style began around 1200. Great British architects include Sir Christopher Wren (1632-1723) who built St. Paul's Cathedral.

Below: **Lincoln Cathedral, one of Great Britain's many fine churches.**

Britain has produced some superb landscape and portrait painters. The most famous landscape painters were J.M.W. Turner (1775-1851) and John Constable (1776-1837). William Hogarth (1697-1764) is known for his paintings and engravings which are critical of the behaviour of people. The modern British sculptor Henry Moore (1898-1986) achieved an international reputation.

British composers include Henry Purcell (1659-1695), who wrote the first major British opera, *Dido and Aeneas.* The operas of Benjamin Britten (1913-1976), such as *Peter Grimes,* are widely performed. The performing arts, particularly music and drama, flourish in Britain and attract many tourists.

Below: ***The Burning of the Houses of Parliament***, a painting by J. W. M. Turner.

Farming

Farmland covers just over three-quarters of Britain. Mountains, forests and cities cover most of the rest of the country. Since 1945, most farmers have adopted modern methods. Farm machinery has replaced the need for many farm workers. As a result, farming now employs only 2.5 per cent of the work force. Yields are high and Britain produces about two-thirds of the food it needs.

Most arable (crop-producing) farms are in the drier, low-lying eastern parts of the country. The main crops are cereals, especially wheat and barley, potatoes and sugar beet. Vegetables and fruits are also important. Greenhouses are used to grow many vegetables, flowers and pot plants.

Below: **Wheat covers a greater area of farmland than any other crop.**

About three-fifths of British farms rear animals, especially cattle and sheep. Beef cattle and sheep are important on hilly land in the west, which is unsuitable for crops. Dairy farming is carried on wherever there is plenty of lush grass. Pigs are reared mainly in eastern and northern England. The production of poultry has been steadily increasing.

Woodland covers about 7 per cent of England, 14 per cent of Scotland and 12 per cent of Wales. However, nearly 90 per cent of Britain's wood is imported.

Fish is an important food. Britain is a major fishing country and its fishing fleet provides about two-thirds of its needs. Fish farming for salmon, trout and shellfish is increasing.

Above: **Scottish fishermen land nets of fish on a trawler.**

Industry

Although some of its traditional industries have declined in recent years, Great Britain remains a major industrial nation. Its leading resource is oil, which comes from rocks under the North Sea. Britain is Europe's chief oil producer. In 1986, it ranked sixth among world producers. Also important are coal and natural gas. These three fuels are used to generate electricity. Nuclear power stations produce about 17 per cent of the electricity supply and some comes from hydroelectric power stations.

Various minerals are mined for building and manufacturing. But most metals, including iron ore, are imported. Despite this, Britain is the world's tenth most important steel producer. Industry, including mining and manufacturing, employs 38 out of every 100 workers.

Below: **Robots are used on modern car assembly lines.**

Steel, which is produced mainly in Wales, Scotland and northern England, is used to make such things as aircraft, vehicles, engines, ships and many kinds of equipment. Other manufactured goods include chemicals and artificial fabrics, textiles, and food and drink. Many industries now use microelectronics and robots. High-technology products include computers and much electrical equipment. Many manufactured products are exported. Britain is the world's fifth most important trading country.

Great Britain also earns money from services, including tourism and financial services, such as banking and insurance. Services employ 59 per cent of Britain's work force.

Below: **Natural gas is burned off at an oil rig in the North Sea.**

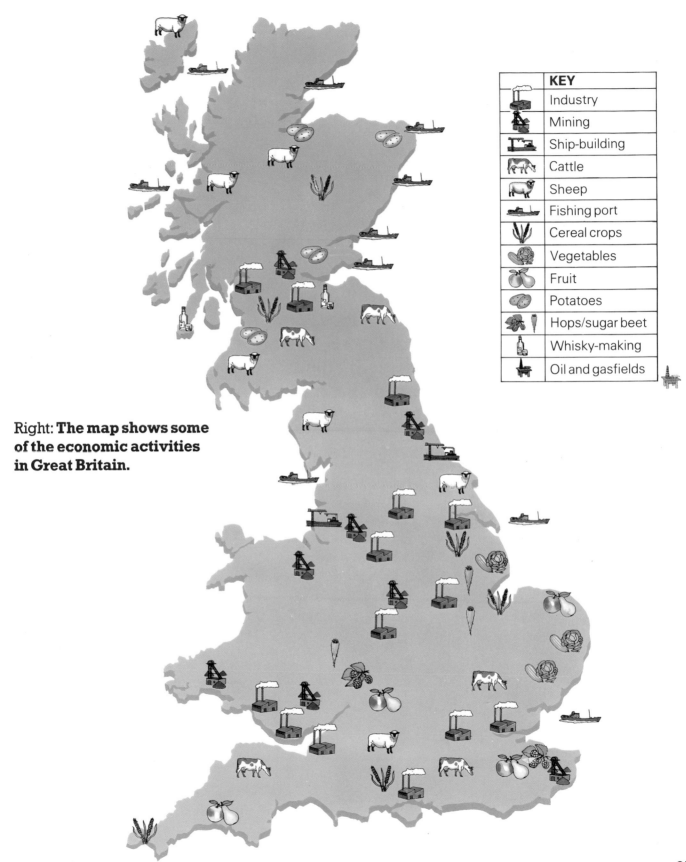

KEY

	Industry
	Mining
	Ship-building
	Cattle
	Sheep
	Fishing port
	Cereal crops
	Vegetables
	Fruit
	Potatoes
	Hops/sugar beet
	Whisky-making
	Oil and gasfields

Right: **The map shows some of the economic activities in Great Britain.**

Looking to the future

Britain has changed greatly in the last 40 years. Its vast empire has become a Commonwealth – a free association of 48 independent countries headed by the British monarch. One factor which binds these countries together is English, the world's leading business language. Britain also plays an important part in the European Economic Community, which it joined in 1973, the North Atlantic Treaty Organization, and in the United Nations.

The country's economy is still changing. Many older industries have declined, partly because of competition from other countries. But new industries, many based on high technology, are replacing older industries.

Below: **A primary school. The British education system is going through many changes at present.**

Above: **The Queen takes part in many ceremonies, such as Trooping the Colour in London. Britain's Royal Family is a unifying force, because it is above party politics.**

Right: **The British people have faced major challenges in recent years, particularly large-scale unemployment following the decline of traditional industries.**

Facts about Great Britain

Area:
229,799 sq km
(88,795 sq miles)

Population:
55,061,000 (1985 est)
(England, 47,112,000;
Scotland, 5,137,000; and
Wales, 2,812,000

Capital:
London

Largest cities:
London (6,775,000)
Birmingham (1,004,000)
Glasgow (725,000)
Leeds (711,000)
Sheffield (534,000)

Official language:
English

Religion:
Christianity

Main exports:
Manufactured goods,
machinery, fuels,
chemicals,
transport equipment

Unit of currency:
Pound

Great Britain compared with other countries

Britain 232 per sq. km.

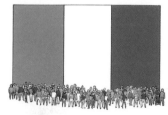

France 100 per sq. km.

USA 26 per sq. km.

Australia 2 per sq. km.

Above: **How many people? Britain is heavily populated compared with many other countries.**

Below: **How large? Britain has a small land area compared with many other countries.**

USA   **Australia**   **France**   **Great Britain**

Below: **British money and stamps: The pound is divided into 100 pence.**

Orkney Islands

Shetland Isles

Outer Hebrides

Isle of Skye

Northern Highlands

Inverness

Monadhliath Mountains

Aberdeen

Moray Firth

SCOTLAND

Isle of Mull

Grampian Mountains

Dundee

R. Forth

Firth of Forth

Atlantic Ocean

R. Clyde

Edinburgh

Glasgow

Firth of Clyde

Southern Uplands

R. Tweed

NORTHERN IRELAND

Newcastle

Carlisle

R. Tyne

Sunderland

R. Tees

Middlesbrough

North Sea

Lake District

Isle of Man

The Pennines

Yorkshire Moors

REPUBLIC OF IRELAND

Irish Sea

Blackpool

York

Hull

Leeds

Manchester

Huddersfield

Liverpool

R. Mersey

Sheffield

Anglesey

Caernarvon

Snowdonia

Stoke-on-Trent

Nottingham

The Wash

Derby

R. Trent

WALES

Wolverhampton

Leicester

Norwich

Cambrian Mountains

Birmingham

Coventry

R. Ouse

Cambridge

ENGLAND

Ipswich

Northampton

R. Usk

R. Severn

Gloucester

Oxford

Chiltern Hills

St George's Channel

Brecon Beacons

Swindon

London

Swansea

Cardiff

Bristol

Reading

R. Thames

North Downs

R. Avon

Bristol Channel

South Downs

Dover

Exmoor

R. Test

Brighton

Taunton

R. Exe

R. Stour

Southampton

Atlantic Ocean

R. Tamar

Portsmouth

Exeter

Bournemouth

English Channel

FRANCE

Dartmoor

Isle of Wight

Plymouth

Scale: 1:3,700,000

0   20   40   60 miles

0   40   80 km

Isles of Scilly

Index

PRINTED IN BELGIUM BY

proost
INTERNATIONAL BOOK PRODUCTION

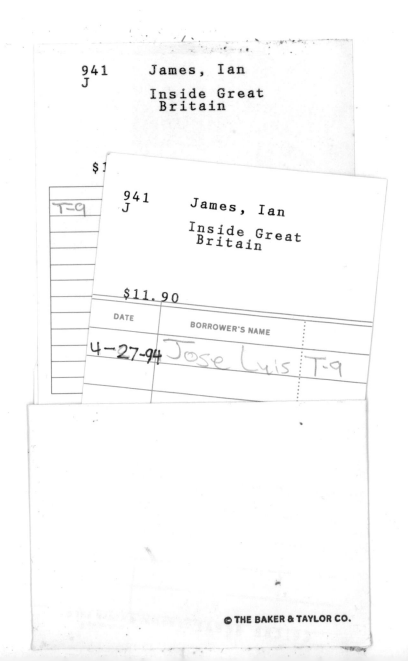

941   James, Ian
J
           Inside Great
           Britain

$1

T-9

941   James, Ian
J
           Inside Great
           Britain

$11.90

DATE	BORROWER'S NAME	
4-27-94	Jose Luis	T-9

© THE BAKER & TAYLOR CO.